Cloudbank Across the Fens

Cloudbank Across the Fens

Leona Graham-Elen

THE BRIDESWELL PRESS

Copyright © by Leona Graham-Elen 2011
Photographs by Leona Graham-Elen & Richard Elen
Leona Graham-Elen has asserted her right
to be identified as the author of this work.

First published in Great Britain in 2011
by The Brideswell Press,
Somersham, Cambridgeshire,
United Kingdom
brideswell.com

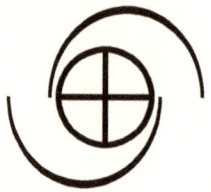

All rights reserved.
No part of this book may be reproduced or transmitted in any form
or by any means—graphic, electronic or mechanical—including
photocopying, recording, or by any information or retrieval system,
without permission in writing from the publisher.

ISBN 978-0-9649553-3-2

First Edition

British Library Cataloguing in Publication Data
A catalogue record for this book is available from the British Library

Printed by Lightning Source

Designed and typeset in Adobe Caslon
by Richard Elen at The Brideswell Press
Cover design by Richard Elen

Table of Contents

Introduction: Spirit of Place vii
Excerpt from *Hereward the Wake* by Charles Kingsley ix

2006

Scots Canadians 1
An Aggregate of Love 3
The Golden Lion At Noon: St Ives, Cambridgeshire.............. 6
The Bright Bird Cage of My Life 8
A Novice in the Fens 10
Cloudbank Across the Fens 11
The Girl Next Door 13
Waterland 14
A Journey in the Fens on 11 March 2006—Notes.................. 15
An Anglian Springtime 17
In the Garden, A Question of Time 17
Journey Home to Scotland 20
Mourning for Ian 21
Malta, Sacred Island 22
Crossing to Godmanchester from Huntingdon 24
Black Birds in the Fog 25
That Black Bird 26
Goddess, Come 27

2007

Tainted 29
The London-Toronto Line: A Winter Train of Thought 30
Welcoming Winter in the Era of Climate Change 31
Planting Primroses in an English Garden 33
A Good Man 34
England, After Canada 35
Fen Magic 36
The Fen Bard 39
The Fentown Ladies 40

2008

Dad's Diary 41
Frida 44
Frida in My Mind 44
Growing All Together in An English Garden 45
Courts of Joy 48
The Swallows of Corfu 49
Owl at Day's End 51

2009

The Great Returning: Sunwards 53

2010

In Memory of John Clare, Fen Poet 54
How Could I Not Love An English Garden Overmuch? 55
Mourning Mother 56
My Sister's Dream 59
Cherry Picking 61
Voices in the Garden 63
Poetry at the End of the World 64
Canada Day, 2010 67
Crimepetitive Capitalism 69
Shades of Green 71
Woman Waiting For A Bus In Oxford 73
The Call of Isis 74
A Year On From Florence's Passing 76

2011

Isis Unveiled, Insh'Allah 77

Introduction: The Spirits of Place

*Genius loci: the distinctive atmosphere
or pervading spirit or guardian deity of a place.*

Like much of my poetry, *Cloudbank Across the Fens* is highly inspired by 'The Spirits of Place' – to wit, Eastern England's fenlands.

Tennessee and the American South inspired my first book of poetry: *At Home In Bell Buckle*. *Moon Over Topanga, Owl in Ojai and Other Tales From Turtle Island* charted the second part of my husband Richard's and my American Adventure – the hot and heady realms of Southern California. Cloudbank sees us 'back home' in Britannia's Magic Isles. Meantime, my country of birth, Canada, in particular Ontario, continues to play a linking role, whilst travels to other European destinations and beyond add to the mix – especially and most recently Egypt.

So, from the lofty mountains of the Santa Monica Range to the temperate low wetlands of Eastern England – our rural village of Somersham, A Giant's Stone's Throw from the Academic Mecca of Cambridge, where the Cam River meanders amid scholars and burghers alike.

The books' titles say *it*; hopefully, the poems sing *it*: messages from The Spirits of Place. Especially in this era of forced endings and brave new beginnings – the end of an unsustainable Old Order that has brought our species near to extinction and the beginning of a New Earth with a new kind of civilization. I may not live to see it, but on the other hand, my mother lived strong for 96 years, so I might – my fingers are permanently crossed for my daughter Kim-Ellen, her partner Colleen and my grandson, Geordy, and all our descendants, that we as a species will rise to the greatest challenge humanity has ever faced, undeniable Climate Change. A deep link exists between Spirit of Place and this human-made catastrophe.

In 1975 I was led to the extraordinary spiritual and ecological Findhorn Community in North East Scotland by legends of community activism, nature spirits, radical thinking ahead of its time. There the reality of The Spirit of Place came home to me. Findhorn's abiding commitment, then and now, is Cooperation with Nature: working together as humans with seen and unseen myriad beings: angels, devas, fairies, nature spirits, gnomes and elementals. There are many ways to see, hear and experience life in its fullness. This drive to work with Nature lead me into the environmental and conservation movement – my favourite email address remains 'at wild.org'.

So here I sit in my Magic Cabin in rural Cambridgeshire, winds gusting and rain pelting down, my familiar Hermes the Cat curled up to my left, the near six-foot sunflower threatening to climb through the kitchen window, the lavender lopped off and harvested and the lemon tree requesting protection against wintery cold – around me The Spirits of Place whisper, cajole, squeak, purr and shout. Nature is One Big Harmony made of Zillions of Notes. *How can we not listen?*

Sadness sometimes overwhelms me as I work on poetry that may outlive our species. On the other hand, poetry is such an ancient art, perhaps the most ancient, along with cave drawings. In our ending is our beginning and a new beginning, so I leave yet another small reckoning with fate.

Leona Graham-Elen
Somersham, Cambridgeshire, England
2010—2011

Introduction

Excerpt from *Hereward the Wake* by Charles Kingsley[1]
From Chapter XX

Hereward takes his mother Lady Godiva from Bourne to Crowland Abbey (a nunnery)/after Normans invaded England/took Bourne/fenlands

And they rowed away for Crowland, by many a mere and many an ea[2]; through narrow reaches of clear brown glassy water; between the dark-green alders; between the pale-green reeds; where the coot clanked, and the bittern boomed, and the sedge-bird, not content with its own sweet song, mocked the song of all the birds around; and then out into the broad lagoons, where hung motionless, high overhead, hawk beyond hawk, buzzard beyond buzzard, kite beyond kite, as far as eye could see. Into the air, as they rowed on, whirred up the great skeins of wild fowl innumerable, with a cry as of all the bells of Crowland, or all the hounds of Bruneswold; and clear above all the noise sounded the wild whistle of the curlews, and the trumpet-note of the great white swan. Out of the reeds, like an arrow, shot the peregrine, singled one luckless mallard from the flock, caught him up, struck him stone dead with one blow of his terrible heel, and swept his prey with him into the reeds again.

---

1 *Thanks to 'Project Gutenberg' for access to this book.*
2 *'ea': river or watercourse (Old English/dialectal).*

Cloudbank Across the Fens

2006

Scots Canadians

On the Occasion of Burns Night: January 2006 in Glastonbury, UK

Scots Canadians.
Generations bred to remember
Born in this world but of another

My father
The Clan Graham

Bonnie Dundee, The Great Montrose
Violence and drama of bygone place and time
Glory bathed in blood
Good or evil measured by broad sword

Rapier or pike
The pipes reminding us
What we lost
What we have to gain
Where we have come
Why we must never forget
N'oublie, our motto
Sundays with the drone of pipes
Sword dances, penny a line
To memorize the immortal bard
Burns himself

My mother
The 'trusty Boyds' to the rescue
Battle of Lags
Beside their King against the Viking hoards
1263, Goldberry Hill
Robert de Boyd remade in my brother Bob

But let us not forget the ladies
For in the old way
The bloodline through them ran
Forward into our time
The plaids mix and match
The right to don them a battle
Lost and won again

Across the seas my people went
Crofts and lands stolen from them
But never honour
Not every chief was noble
My father remembered
They took away the land from The People
You do not take away the land inside The people
They remember the land, the blood spilt

They will keep track
As the grey buildings of Old Paisley
Float behind them in the morning mist
Their hunger great but hopes greater
They leave behind guardians, high and low
Knowing their children's children would return
To claim back with their descendants
From the English and the sheep
The tartan, the land, just governance
All in good time

An Aggregate of Love

To Ian with love from sister Leona
9 February 2006

It took your whole lifetime and 55 years of my own
To constitute the whole of our aggregate.
It shall not fall apart by Death's Dominion
Though I mock not Death. One dares not.
It came so sudden and unbidden upon you.

The memories crowd in,
Massed into a dense cluster.

Aunt Thel's so often there in old photos, standing guard.
Second mother, little did we know her betrayal of the first
Till time told all. So I was little Thel, standing near you,
Making sure you was a happy kid.
You the little one we all adored, the last.
We played together a lot, maybe too much.
I suppose I strove for dominion over your soul and mind
As I watched Ralph train your Olympic physique.
You resented us all in differing degrees; you left it in writing.
But you loved us all outstandingly, too much maybe.

A mixture of minerals separable by mechanical means.
Death breaks us up and down.
Yet the mixture also includes spirit, soul substance,
Love that permeates the cosmos. Divine alchemy.
You are far away these days,
Busy in the supermarket in the sky
As my goddess daughter Meggie said,
Meeting up with old friends,
Comparing notes and life paths and a'that.

But you promised last night
You'd meet me too when I came through the gate
Like Dad said he would
…and I suspect Aunt Thel too…
…it's a mystery, but maybe souls re-form on purpose into old selves
To greet the newest ancestors on the block.
We did indeed aggregate
This family of many parts
For a brief happysad time
When you passed.
We are getting back to normal now
But not really, it will never be the same again.
You were the last to come and damn it,
Wrongly the first to go.
Maybe you had work up there to do.
You were the great athlete though Robert still runs and Ralph still sails.
You were the high jumper who could have gone all the way
But your competitive spirit tackled the spiritual path
And there you outdistanced us all, even me, who pushed you there.

As I played our Scots ancestral music by your deathbed
And you peeped into the white light place
Whence you returned now and then to chide us,
I felt that aggregate of love you forged,
The boy who would be king, your inception
The last real blessing Dad gave us before he died.

2006

The Book of Your Life shows your passage through:
The cute boy turns truly handsome man
And then, after Bloomfield NB, you suddenly fade
For Death had caught you beside McCain's poisonous potato fields.
You aged before us all; it was a terrifying few years.
Moments of love and light and wisdom were there
But we were confused by the Old Man who'd replaced the Boy King.
You fought hard on all levels for life and meaning.
You won, we got the Message, brother: love conquers all.
Death shall have no Dominion.
As Big Brother said, 'Save a few places up there for us'

Ian and Leona, mid-1950s, at '540' in London Ontario

The Golden Lion At Noon: St Ives, Cambridgeshire
10 February 2006

Usually
I come mid morning or afternoon
For a fair decent latte
Full now at noon, the handsome young servers aglow
With work to do
An older couple, drinking their pint, smiling, curious,
Enjoying the mix.

An old-fashioned pub, upgraded
Automatic doors where once the carriages cantered in
A deep peachy continental look
Two flat screens above the bar
Playing pop music videos
(One up from sports)
And the essential espresso machine

That stout man nearby in a pale modish blue jumper
Touch too old for his lady-friend, did he but know it
Behind me a table-full of just barely legal kids
A smart suited looking young business man passes by, but nonetheless sees me
As he notices everything else,
On the way up as he hopes
The cool bar manger with unbelievable sideburns

The couple get up, carefully, donning coats
Over creaking joints
Now I know about those
Slow process
Their day half drunk.
What will follow?
This was a highlight.

The unusable fireplace
Stacked with real uniform logs

2006

A touch of new style grace
Maybe-pretend wooden rafters, reminder of an older look
Vaguely backed up by the polished wood-paneled bar fittings
The un-seeable too small prints on the wall
A mistake

Two older ladies go by, canes to the ready
An eager day to face yet, lots to be done.
A tasty young lad kitted out in the latest T shirt
Wanted it says
The usual sloppy joe trooper trews
His girlfriend in thick stripes
The bright-wheeled game of fortune lit up behind them

The two young'uns behind the bar
Slim and gorgeous in official black
Only the bar manager wears white

The screens announce in red
Welcome to the Golden Lion

Young muscled Wanted orders at the bar
His hair so perfectly casual
This look takes expertise

The Cromwell Room –
A delightful room, we are told.
He'd rise from his grave, musket in hand
Aghast at the decadence of it all
That former St Ives school boy
A Huntingdonshire man
Who turned Britain on his spit
But hail ho, parliament and democracy
Came out of this Golden Lion town

Never underestimate the English
Or the produce from a small market town.

The Bright Bird Cage of My Life
for Robert, Big Brother
22 February 2006

The Soul calls
Speaks to me of many matters
To make me quake
At the root of being
As my stem shudders in the winter wind

Up from the Unconscious
A place of plenty, dark in my burning imagination
A phrase whispered in my inner ear
At night, as sleep eludes me
..the bright bird cage of my life..

The rational mind says
Naturally, all human life is so
A prison designed by endless cultural
Adjustments, to keep the Id in order
To formulate civilization as we know it

Nonetheless, the Soul is My Bird
In This cage and She would sing
And fly to the heavens
Not have clipped wings
And stale bird seed

The door opens at Will
But She would not fly free
Lest loss of all She holds dear
A little bit of both please
Cake and eat it too. Marie Antoinette.

All very well to advise
The simple life
No life is simple

No advice adequate
Free will is always too much to bear

This is humanity
Groans the prisoner
Under Buddha's tree
The price we paid for eternity
Jesus smiles

To fly or not to fly
This is not the question
We can but sing in the cage
Of what would be IF
And we do fly in the end

So brother Ian flew his cage
I saw him do it
He had been practicing days before
Instructing mother and me
To wear white, then we could join him

All we can do is make the cage
Bright, fade the bars
Hold the door open with sharp beak
Eat now and then
Keep it clean

We made this, we can unmake
We see what we choose
A carousel of pain and pleasure
The circus sounds, the monkey music
Bears dancing and snakes charmed

Shall we not sing, then
Of what Life is
Nonetheless, a bright phantom
Passing quickly in the dark night of all time
I shall rejoice

A Novice in the Fens
After Edward Storey, author of Spirit of the Fens
2 March 2006

The move from Huntingdon
Was wise, brought us closer in
For a good look
But the feel of the fens
Breathing the air, digging earth,
Is a deeper matter

The fen tigers
Hide in the hearts
Of these proud people-
A tribe, says Storey, disappearing
As roads and noise, the latest modernities,
Puncture the landscape

The mix of blood potent
Ancient Brit-but no longer beaker folk,
So-called Celt, Angle, Saxon, Jute and Dane,
Viking hoards, Norman,
Even German POWs who stayed
Incomers all, tamed by The Land

Heroes, depending on your watch,
Like Hereward the Wake,
Robin Hood of his time,
Of all classes, but the man and woman
In the long flat fields, feet firm
In dark rich moist soil, they stand still

From out the confines of past time
Whispers in the reed beds
Skylark song, a windy chorus
On a cold day, a crumbling church,
A towering abbey, flooded fields,
They tell the tale

Each landscape has its spirit
Nature and human hand and time passing
Make it so, we are animals and we are earth
We return to the fields and run in the rivers
But we also sing in the soul's journey
Outward and beyond, returning and re-turning

Cloudbank Across the Fens

Upon reading Mary Chamberlain's Fenwomen *(Virago, 1975)*
5 March 2006

End of day across cold fens, dank winter winds,
Clutch of cloud streaks grey violet over magnolia, pink, pale blue.

Cloudbank looming in the distance.
Brought to mind
How sky meets cloud.
Horizons, dark and light
Edges, things banked up, stored,
Differences, despair.
Being up against it.
The whole shebang.

Fenwomen of past times, through an hourglass.
Men still make more, the raven sings.
Options limited, despite the vote, other women's liberation.
Up against it, you can bank on that.

Mary's list of little girls: what will you be when you grow up?
Hairdresser wins, teacher second-best,
Or happy to keep house like mum.
But Fiona hoped to be a horse trainer.
Long ago, Lily Levitt, 83 in 1974,
Rode astride and got away with it.
Seems easier now,
Still, isolation in this island kingdom, fear of strangers.
Wonder what they'll say in another 100 years?
We all watch the long slow dark clouds ride across the fens.

Such a sad set of tales,
A hard grind, poverty dark and biting.
Tying celery, tending beet root, gleaning, in service,
Laying out dead skylarks for Londoners to eat,
Growing flowers for Covent Garden Market,
Long walks back and forth to work across the darkling fens,
Fleeting moments of pleasure,
Death and funeral at Church or Chapel.
But then there's Aida Hayhoe
Who stayed up to darn and mend,
Despite husband calling her to bed,
Waited till he fell sound asleep.
She had three whilst others begat 14, even 21
Quite a cloudbank.

The Girl Next Door
For L
11 March 2006

The girl next door
Is a fenwoman
For certain.
She knows this village,
Its people and measure.
Born and raised
Out of the dark rich soil,
Here where reeds sing
In concert with skylark.

Everything she touches
Changes, like goddess of old
For the better,
Moves forward into productivity,
Be it garden or allotment,
Lives of those she loves.
She commands my allegiance.
Again, I become
Lady-in-waiting.

Golden-haired, bright eyed
She watches over her domain,
Our common benefactress
How can we but love her?
Pure heart and winged justice,
She follows in the footsteps
Of ancient forbears.
I can but watch and take her lead
As I stumble through the magic of her land

Waterland

After reading Graham Swift's novel 'Waterland'
19 March 2006

What spirit possessed this Swift
To such a height of fictional fury
If not Storey's very same Spirit of the Fens
A tale where even fenland ale plays
A key part, where each part of the puzzle
Locks into another, a story of locks and keys, sluices
Windmills, waterways, incest
History lessons, natural and otherwise
Repeating themselves
Of men and eels, bad luck, dredger and silt
Will o' the wisp, ghostly Mary Atkinson
Madness or no, choices made in
The Here and Now

A Journey in the Fens on 11 March 2006—Notes
with Richard

1. Somersham to Sutton-in-the-Isle: went to church (pepperbox type) read about in Edward Storey, *Portrait of the Fens:* St Andrew's (CofE). Stone statues of St Ethelreda and St Andrew. Talked briefly with priest, as did Richard. Church built as part of reward for people there who helped gather/deliver stone for Ely Cathedral, often visible in distance from roundabout there….as Sutton is on a hill. Met local woman—a white woman born in Pakistan—who guided us around the church and told us something of background of village: very few older buildings left, thanks to development, etc. Told us about prisoners of war (Civil?) nearby so we went out and found in Sutton Gault, including the lovely Anchor Inn, which often gets isolated by watery fens; will go to dinner there on 29th. The area is much more watery and fen-like than Somersham and south, masses of watery fields and canals, the two Bedford rivers (old and new…).
2. Thru Wardy Hill, Coveney to Pymoor-to B1411 that runs alongside 'The Hundred Foot Washes', a very long straight road. Stopped at old drainage station where there was a poem on old building about water as 'the foe'. Went up to top of the dams that hold back the waters (canals/drainages) and saw the watery landscape….
3. Across Wash at Welney to Tipps End, to Manea where Charles 1st was going to build a place complex (re Storey) much to amusement of the folks there; saw a newish estate road called Charlemont—what he was going to name it! Then to Purls Bridge and Welches Dam, where we went into RSPB and Woodland Trust reserve and visited inside a hide (will go again when warmer!).
4. Back past Manea up thru Wimblington/alongside of March on small roads thru Tholomas Drove (lots of droves…), Parson Drove (saw one called Adventurers Drove…), Church End, Throckenholt to Crowland Abbey (Croyland originally). Went into town first (parked in Abbey parking lot) and saw

'Trinity' Bridge, very old fashioned leftover (R: photos), and then to George and Angel pub (pic of stain glass window, R) as I had peeked in and though smokey, welcoming and interesting old fashioned pub. Had Guiness and crisps. Guy lent us Abbey book but we also had Storey at hand. Read about Crowland and then to impressive Abbey remains. Alongside, a parish church 'remained'…large graveyard, lots of good angles….impressive arch (decorative)…story of St Guthlac and his hard times founding it (originally wattle type buildings), maybe 3 foundings.

5. Up to Spalding but did not investigate…will come again in tulip season (festival). Back via Crowland and Thorney. Saw a beautiful small white owl.

An Anglian Springtime
17 May 2006

It didn't simply spring up this year
(Please forgive the poor pun)
It teased our wintered senses, rushed back,
Played warm and cold and in between
It now sweeps through, glorious bounty in its wake

It may serve or not to name its elements
Perhaps its overwhelming beauty demands
It be appeased by the inexpressible
Penultimate blooming words
It outweighs the clever mind

In any case, the bluebells ring out their spell
Quixotic, the starry woodruff, Old French *mug-de-boys*
Its lost healing magic imparts, beneath
Purple lilac, white clematis gone wild and ivy green
An ancient fuchsia bush recovers from a serious trim

In the Garden, A Question of Time
15 June 2006

In the garden
They speak to me, the myriad unseen
Embodied in every plant, flower and weed,
Vegetable and herb, a rush of life
Making life, creating forms beautiful and useful,
Keeping us alive, coating the planet,
A gorgeous dress-up by Mother Nature
Who dances with the Great God Pan.
I have heard His Pipes and seen Her Face

Leona in her Somersham garden

In the garden
I have hope, the birds sing subtle songs
About mundane matters, the roses glitter
And the sky darkens, the moon makes rings,
The Evening Star reminds me
The White Queen watches over me.
Every breath I take stems from The Sacred
Around and about, within and without,
How can I doubt, it is only a question of time.

We are never not in the garden.
If wise, we would tend it well, lest we too
Become bird-food underfoot, our time cut short.
We may tend our ailing roses whilst oceans die,
Forests crumble, fresh water drains away
And species disappear, but we must take our pitchfork
To the inner garden of mind and soul, grow there
Resolve, solutions to heal the planet now,
Our greed the evil scourge we must root out

In the garden
The gods speak
Goddess listens.
We have played at dominion.
Let us wake at dawn
And become as angels,
Spades and forks our wings
It is only a question of time
In the garden

Journey Home to Scotland
15 June 2006

It's only a day's journey
Through northern mountains and vales,
Including stopping by Killiecrankie
To deliver Ian's ashes up to his ancestors,
Where Bonnie Dundee beat the English
When the sun glinted off their armour.

It's not a long journey on the ground
Through glory of bluebell and blackthorn,
Rooks calling me home.
But we travel different dimensions,
Far from round busy tones and towns of England
Into landscapes where old dreams still come true.

The broad sweep of Moray highland
Against wide firth, all green and gold,
A fruitful land, with oil to top it off;
Touches of wilderness mixed with farming,
A patina of tourism glossing this horn of plenty,
A country set to break your heart.

Old spirits watch over, as The Land
Returns to descendants denied and mocked,
Their plaids and flags once again flying bold
Against blue grey skies.
Even the English are proud of being Scottish
Right down to the Queen through her mam.

Mourning for Ian
29 June 2006

Each day
Clouds cover my grief
As the gap in my heart
Bleeds blue sky.

The English garden comforts me:
    Late winter whites,
        Yellows, purples, spring up in Eostre's memory,
        Pinks, reds, as summer blooms
        At the height of Pan's delight, all rise in his honour.
    The old-fashioned pale pink fuchsia bush
    Resplendent, fulsome after a bitter trim.
    Overgrown lilac blue ceanothus awaits its turn,
    Resurgent rosy mallow fills my window to the world.
    Roses, reds, pinks, whites, yellows, fly flags of honour.

That well-fed blackbird trundles by,
An occasional startling magpie,
Plucky pigeons, starlings, thrushes, tits.

They pass through
As we all do.
They return, same but different
Like we will.

Malta, Sacred Island
November 2006

We were warned
About its dry and dusty nature.
We found her balmy and damp
Under a bright November sky,

Tourists lumbering through narrow passages,
Towering golden masonry shimmering in the sunlight
Over inquisitive forays by jeep and foot.
An ancient, tired island, but always open for business.

Officially European by necessity, Euros impending,
Old Melita takes us further back than any other land
To our megalithic roots, older by far
Than Egypt's pyramids or England's Stonehenge.

Ggantija, Hagar Qim, Mnajdra, Tarxien, Ta'Hagrat, Skorba.
As above so below: the Hypogeum.

Telling temples, speaking stone, oracles intact
Remembering who we once were:

A peaceful people, builders, pastoralists
Honouring female and male alike,
Round fecund images of females
Predominate, awake, asleep, alive, now

Disappearing into a gap in time,
Followed by Phoenicians, sea trade wizards
Bearing enduring gifts of blood and tongue
Then, inevitably, Romans, Turks and Christian knights.

War, urbanization, religion, sins of the fathers,
A greedy Napoleon, Britain to the rescue,
The George Cross for resisting the invading Hun
The Maltese Cross flies again from St Angelo.

A long bloody history decimated by German bombs.
They survive, emerge from underground mazes,
Hewn from the same soft stone their ancestors
Moulded into temples under the same steely stars,

Into a blessed Mediterranean sun,
To reconstruct stunning churches and cathedrals
Across a rocky skyline against an azure sea
Village and city prosper, the people pray.

So quietly, the temples remain,
From over thirty-five hundred years ago
Long before Jehovah or Allah
The sacred builders spoke in stone

About a better way to live.
We search these living rocks
To better understand
What could be.

If Only.

Crossing to Godmanchester from Huntingdon
13 December 2006

An old bridge between the two.
1266 the plaque boasts.
It's always a windy walk
With the Great Ouse streaming below,
Teams of swans in tow,
Flocks of black-feathered birds above.

There's something about the crossing…
Mid-river you pass over in time.
When you catch your breath,
Whatever the season, you're gone
With the faeries, they touch your soul
You barely make it back, whichever way

Someone, sometime, way back when
Laid a spell upon the crossin
As belike they be lookin into this day
An hour, a hole in hourglass
I swears, I feel grey rags blow round me
A kerchief red upon me head.

I'm glad to be over.
I check my watch for lost minutes
And breathe easier for the time bein
But maybe I needs be more careful even
As something carries through each time
I am never the same after crossing

Black Birds in the Fog
22 December 2006

The fog holds
Us in its freezing grasp
But black birds of all sorts
Gather on rooftops
Adorning aerials and chimneys
Lined up in order
The largest, the highest and the loudest

A stillness enfolds
All but them, they converse too
In bare branches against grey skies
They flit from house to house
Street to street. They discuss us
And like us, the weather
Endlessly happily eerily

The big birds at Heathrow
Are in go slow mode
But here in the fens
Black birds remember other fogs
There is something about a fog
They like, a mystery their genes carry,
Evermore

That Black Bird
24 December 2006

That black bird
Claims as his own
Our small but lovely garden green

Golden beaked
He flits about
Grabbing all the goodies on the ground

He seems to smile
And look my way
When I watch him from my kitchen safe

Painstakingly he pops
Here and there
Back-dropped by budding snowdrop and primrose

Starling and thrush
Have little to say
Somehow he knows he will have his way

He teaches
Persistence
Like winter when you think it's passed

Black against white
Today he called
To say, watch me, bird of all seasons

And I laughed
To see his golden beak
And black body just where I want him

Goddess, Come
24 December 2006

In these days when the gods of a merely recent past
Stir from their graves
Jehovah Jesus and Mohammad
Watching their devotees
Descendants of the desert fathers
Pray for Armageddon
As they battle out old patriarchal feuds
Goddess, Come

We sing our song
Blackbirds bright against blue sky
Wheel and dip into green canopies
Re-membering ourselves
Before they were, we were.
A black masculinity covers their women
Some praise the prisons they embrace.
Goddess, Come, Liberate

When we were younger
We said it was the last gasp of the patriarchy
A long drawn out battle-cry
From the wounded heart of men
And women born from their broken ribs
Religion as evil, death-driven
Endless fields of yellow stars, crosses and crescents
Goddess, Come, Liberate Them

We had thought we were progressing well
But our task has hardly begun
Our song must reach a deeper pitch, a higher tone
Before Gaia turns against this plague of humans
Let us align with Her in humility and courage
Listen to the Magic Words hidden in
The Valley of the Light of Life
Goddess, Come, Liberate Us

Phillipa Bowers' sculpture at home in our Somersham garden

2007

Tainted
10 January 2007

Walking the lake yesterday
Spring winds in wintertime
Confusion of blossom
And shoots in January
Revelation

Tainted by base desire
Glamour, fame and fortune
Eluding me as I age
Ungracefully, unwillingly
Remember

The jolly adventuress
Come home to roost
In awkward security
This cannot be allowed
Resistance

Innocence
Flew long ago
Life hurls forward
Return to wildness
Required

Faery wings flash
Against the cage of my undoing
Old eyes drop and new
Now I see Love
Requited

The London-Toronto Line: A Winter Train of Thought

On my daughter Kim-Ellen's birthday – 16 February 2007

Paragraphs of snow, periods of trees
End with a statement: a fractured family
Pose a question
Mark how the memory of death of the youngest brother and son
Repeats the pain in the eye of the heart
A drifting sadness creeps over all

Lines of agri-structures, Ontario's baseline
Forward through the shining glint of blowing snow
Hanging wires
Crossing frozen rivers high above on trusting tracks
Brantford now, black branches
Against sun-parked automobiles, 25 below and dropping

Gullies, hills and stubble-filled cornfields
Pale grey water towers and grain silos
Bush and black crows, ravens waiting, watching
Stretch oil tankers, yellow school buses, red trailer trucks
File by, beside the train on the 401
Sun haloed through glass bauble street lights

Southern Ontario, the frontier feel of it:
Cold white cement blocks grey rust brick bloated barn buildings
Rocks wilderness snow-banked hills. Trees. Surviving.
The People: polite, reserved, thoughtful, careful.
The man behind says "I am what I am" to his thrifty wife,
A grade above other North Americans, I am grateful to be one.

Light and shade across spruce and pine
The woman beside me is quiet in her beige white-checkered coat
Whilst two black horses look our way, grazing in white-brown fields.
The story ends at Toronto Central, we step down into the big cold
metal box of a station.

Still, the pain remains: the paragraphs, the sentences, the words,
   the letters
Of a life gone to death and a family splitting its infinity.

Welcoming Winter in the Era of Climate Change
Cambridgeshire, England. Winter Solstice 2006.

*In honour of Dr Ian Player and my wilderness conservationist
colleagues, our planetary 'A Team'.
Presented at Birthday Gala for Dr Ian Player, London, UK.
8 March 2007*

Summer surprised some. A long autumn too. And now, the second
   warmest winter.
A deep fog descends. Hoar frost delineates clear and present designs.
Pale peachy skies follow faint blue foggy vistas across sleeping fens.
A rogue robin, voting against Malta, suspecting an early spring,
Pokes the crusty earth, wondering at *my* procrastination.

We the people welcome winter's fall for fear of worse to come.
Winter will not keep us warm in these waste-lands.
Is there time to turn the ghastly tide of our desires?
We scramble to rationalize what we use, how and for how long
We can get away with it. *Hurry up please, it's time.*

This Season of Dark fading to Light feels different.
There's more to do than simply change to eco light bulbs
Or gather naked gifts for those you love to save the trees.
New Year's resolutions demand global dimensions.
We face the sins of our forefathers, our grandmothers' mistakes

Our mothers' greed, our fathers' fears, the wrath of the old gods.
Our own helplessness. A terrible legacy to our children.
The time is out of joint. The robin worries along with the wee wren.
The polar bear struggles in the far north, soon to disappear
   with the ice.

Cloudbank Across the Fens

The Queen of Dolphins died yesterday.
May the white rhino stay safe.

All around us they scream for help as one by one
A species shuts its last eyes for the last time.
We huddle in the muddle we have made.
This is the greatest bloody ball game there's ever been
And the serve is in our court. *Hurry up please, it's time.*

Goonight. Goonight all. Goonight. Ta ta. Goonight.
Good night, ladies and gentlemen, good night, good night, good night.

Planting Primroses in an English Garden
23 March 2007

The creamy white primroses with orange eyes
Caught my attention, demanded my trust
And with them, the depleted orange pansies
Now alert and pert in the ground across from their pals.

They are all in league with one another.
Planting one lot nearby purple and yellow-eyed cousins
Worrying about how they'd get on—it's clear
They know what they want, where and who they want to be.

The daffodil bulbs placed in the autumn
They too said, here, no here, not there, silly.
And where I put tulips as told, they've come up.
There's something about an English Garden.

The mints have minds of their own, random indeed,
Two types of parsley battle it out, side by side,
Rosemary keeps watch over all, never mind thyme,
And all the lavenders have taken me for a ride.

When something's not wanted, it dies or breaks
Other guys get a look-in then, there's room
But who knows who'll join in next
In my most magical English Garden?

Well, for a start, maybe olives and lemons
But only if I look after our cherry better.
Last year the enemy got her when we were busy
Doing photo-duty for Open Garden Day

A good English Garden has a soul,
The one you place in there with your own
Its personality changes but the soul
Reaches out beyond the grave, *alive alive oh!*

A Good Man
For C – July 2007

A good man
Deserves no platitude
Sterling praise perhaps
His worth in gold

He stands firm
The best of neighbours
The prize fighter
The one who holds the line

He's fought our battles
Died for our sins
Paid the price
Knowing all along

Who's who and why
The deep injustice
Of class, money
The whole he-bang

Well, we good women
Salute you as we bear you
Birth, raise, marry and bury you
Beside ourselves with love

England, After Canada
26 Oct 2007

Returning

    My world turned tiny once again, leaves less colorful
    Tree-lines thin and scantier, vistas smaller
    Boxed in, tied up, ducks in a row

Remembering

    Daily long distance journeys, no sweat
    Lake Ontario, Lake Sinclair, Lake Michigan
    Let alone Lake Huron, vast horizons

Recalling

    Burning August days, sweet September bliss, October falls
    In the end, red and gold strewn carpet for my farewell.
    I fell in love again, O Canada

Rehashing

    Times spent with family and old friends, people
    Too present a broader spectrum
    Across the miles right and left wave memories

Fen Magic
26 October 2007

Fen magic lies
    In the long sweeping lines and curves
       encompassing this looking glass wonderland
Hawk hovering, sea gull diving, black crow calling
    In memories alive, ghosts of times past,
       striding across deep dark peaty fields
Hard labouring, making most of very little, defending ditch and field

It wraps itself around the unwilling heart, takes in the unsuspecting,
   traps the unwanted.
It claims that which will advance its best line of defence

      We the People belong to The Land
         Our mirror deceives
            The planet will endure
     We come and go to serve
        The natural order
           The mirror cracks

2007

This water wonder land,
Turned at great cost to cropland by Royal Will and cunning
     Dutchmen
Into a Land of Plenty, England's kitchen garden.
Returned, so easily, to wetland, a natural flow between land and sea,
It sustains us at its will. We would do well to watch our step.

Once upon another time
     A tribal people whose dna descendents live amongst us
     Honoured harmony of sky, water and land in sacred rite.
     Here at Flag Fen we walk in their footsteps, their spirits rest
     here still.
     Be ware the fleeting glimpse at the corner of your eye, no
     hawk descending.

All time is Now
     A flow of vision, of high intent where space and matter meet.
     Turn fast enough and all will be revealed.
     As above so below, so they gave their best
     To the watery under realms whence we all descend.

The magic turns in our blood and spins with the wind
It begs to be seen and known and used for the glory of old gods and
     new.
All gods are one and none; it is what we make of magic
That counts—super natural, extra ordinary.

The long flat landscapes, watery vistas, gushing rivers, tree lines that
     speak,
The weaving corn and thick smell of verdure, sweet water meadows,
The full sky piled with cloudbanks, fields of bright tulips, sunny
     daffodils
All this openness, this lightness, a magic message from Creation.

The Fen Bard
7 November 2007

He strides
>> Across the wooden walkway
>> To this sacred isle, shadowy beast beside,
Above, dun bird of prey, awing

He swings
>> A robust staff in powerful grip
>> Dark, sculpted face aglow
Wan winter sunlit filt'ring through cloudy sky

He will sing
>> Of times present, past and future
>> Of life deeper than human skin
Clouds roll back for this son of Man to reason why

His people
>> Follow wordlessly, equal every one
>> Eager, silent, awe-full with no fear,
Of he who is the bard, not priest or king

His word
>> Their bible nonetheless
>> They read with care, hear his tone,
Inflection, how elements round him beckon

He holds
>> Their memories, bloodlines, meaning
>> Before time collapses into clockwork
They watch, remember to each dying day

This poesy
>> Brings understanding, no incomprehension,
>> Springs from heart and mind
Intellect commanded by the soul, awake

The Fentown Ladies
23 November 2007

The Fentown Ladies
And a few Sirs by the way
Dance in a Court of Mysteries

Book in hand we waltz to a tune of our own
Some display magic power
Disguised as praise above all

Little Ms Horner sat in the corner
Processing books till she's blue
What else for her to do?

But some be
Off to London see the Queen
For tea and cakes in a palace scene

We have Her approval
Our just reward
But who is to say what will happen today

Take this book or that--off with its head!
Enough to send pawns back to our bed
Or champions be, but make sure it's read

I could carry on till day's early dawn
Or meet the White Rabbit in town
But who is to say what will happen today

Best be off to the Court to help them sort
For do we dream of the day
When we have our own castle in play

We can pile our books as high as the sky
No worry about empty slots by and by
For we will have won the play of the day

2008

Leona with her father Alex Graham, at '540' in 1958

Dad's Diary
29 January 2008

Christmas 1960: I give Dad a journal to do a Diary for the year. I write "…I will take it—and keep it—and cherish it as a living part of you—left to me—for the rest of my life—in it will be your philosophy of life & perhaps—episodes to exemplify it—so please Poppa—This isn't kid stuff."

It came true
A kind of karmic nightmare
Haunting me now, 47 years later
As I transcribe *it* into Word format
For whom, and why
It's hard to say

I tried to lose it
But found again
Amongst my sweet dead brother's books
Annotated here and there
By 'Mother', it is as alive
As it was, when written, day by

Excruciating day
Telling me things
I never wanted to hear
His unhappiness
His failure to make it
In this world

The streets of Toronto
Its pain and depths
Of degraded capitalism
The social worker's
Hopeless unwelcome task
To make better what cannot

His inevitable decline
A falling away
From grace, from a
Happy War
Where he was welcome
Wars were made for him, he said

Post war hell
Hitler-was-right
Chant of despair
Blaming others, himself, the eldest,
Pots calling kettles black
Over inextinguishable fires

Clinging onto hope
Having lost the elder girl
To an enemy he never faced

2008

Yet reading psychology
To make a grade, only to fail
Even one entry a day is too much

I fear to open the worn green cover
To uncover yet more pain
He must have known
All the days of my life
This has indeed returned
To make me see, better

Who and where and why
We all were what we are
He saw his death coming
It stalked his days
Like the youngest
Old before his time

We live on
The rest of us
All of us
Even Mum
94 and counting
And the eldest beat the odds

We turn back
And see him
Solitary in his rented room
Dimes and nickels piled
No spare dollars
All he left was thirty cents

He wanted Home
But couldn't make or keep it
The gift he gave
Was Big Love
He wasn't really a bad guy
He'd just outlived His War

Frida

Edited by Penn Kemp, 25 Feb 2008

When a bus and tram collided
A new particular pain commenced
The harness and nails
Protrude from the past
Graphically pulling me to you
Putting mere things in perspective
You peer into my soul
I become lost in your eyes
Your hands hold me too
Like you my eyebrows
Once met, lusty we were
Passion abiding
The Goddess of Old Mexico
Sings shrill and sweet
The monkeys play
The black cat watches

Frida in My Mind

24 February 2008

All my life
You have been there.
When you died in 1954
I was 12: when you were 12
A bus and tram collided
A new particular pain commenced
The harness and nails
Protrude from the past
Graphically demanding
Pulling me to you
Putting mere things in perspective
You peer into my soul

I did not know you at first
But when I did
I became lost in your eyes
Your hands hold me too
The Goddess of Old Mexico
Sings shrill and sweet
The monkeys play
The black cat watches
Like you my eyebrows
Once met, lusty we were
Passion abiding alma mater
You made way for us to come

Growing All Together in An English Garden
27 April 2008

In my garden
I have planted many a good
Herb, flower, vegetable, tree and shrub—
In the dark sticky fen soil they
Squirm their way lightwards
Suck up the rain
Suffer from slugs and wayward bugs
And not least,
My misunderstanding of what's best.
Most of all they sing

In my garden
Rosemary's tale's so fulsome
She's drowned out the Sage.
Mints still talk amongst themselves,
Butting up against Thyme and Oregano.
Lavender struggles to get an edge,
Oddly. Parsley needs training.
Heartsease hides under an assumed name.
Chives wonder where Garlic got to.
All in all, a mixed choir

In my garden
Tulips dance and daffs tango.
Bluebells, grape hyacinth and other purples
Hold the royal standard high
Gladioli wait their turn.
Anemones pop up for a breath of fresh air.
Roses remain constant, in memory of a past dispensation,
Pelargonium winter over well,
Pansy and primrose hold their ground
All sweet-voiced, pandemonium

In my garden
Lettuces, red and green,
And other frail plugs from fen farms
Sit in neat rows hoping for the best
In a lawn recently converted
Not entirely convinced it will work,
With trays and pots of radishes, onions
And such like sprouting, waiting their turn
In the soil-improved earth
All seem nervous, though willing

In my garden
The ancient pink fuchsia sighs in shock.
Forsythia took pruning better.
The clematis eternal, passion flower put out,
Climbing white roses can be counted on.
Lilac unhappy, ivy incorrigible,
Jasmine and other as yet unidentified potentates,
Those purple-flowering whatever, robust
Wild strawberries spring up, inedible crab apples toss.
A wild rhapsody sweeps through all

In my garden
A two-trunk self-rooted infant Maple of some sort
Insists on making itself heard, begging for life
Whilst far to the back the cherished Cherry
Blossoms, welcoming its newly arrived cousin
Apricot, both askance at troubled Fig

2008

They all wonder where in the hell is Apple
But really put out by tarty Lemon
Far too cosseted by half
They all agree

In my garden
Black Cat Hermes guards these troops
From Alfie and other McCavity-types.
Yellow eyes like sunflowers yet to come;
The inherited gnome sits in state .
Margaret's pregnant fairy watches.
In the arbor the White Queen holds court,
Analyzing the Gardener's ability
Kindly, methinks, she seems to wink
All considered, what a band
Growing all together in an English Garden

Courts of Joy
May 15 2008

I entered into the Courts of Joy
Without my knowing exactly
Why
The doors opened
I was within

There are no limits
Once you pass the gates
I am amazed
How easy it is
After all

Remembering to forget
Forgetting to remember
What constitutes a peak moment
Contentment, nowness
All or some and more

Listing negatives and positives
Says nothing or too much
There's ecstasy
But that has been so diminished
Wonderment, maybe

I shall meet you
There, where the fountain sings
Beside the apple orchard
Merry Meet Merry Part
And Merry Meet Aguin

The Swallows of Corfu
24 July 2008

On 4 July 2008 Richard and I went to Corfu for a magical week. Richard gave a series of lectures on 'Ambisonics' at the Department of Music at the Ionian University, whilst I finally had the opportunity to visit this famed island, so rich in history, a haven for creative people, the source of conservationist/writer Gerald Durrell's lifelong dedication to nature, and a potent early base for his older brother novelist/poet/travel writer Lawrence. Although marred by tourism, Corfu continues holds onto its innate Magic, an amalgam of many cultures, for example, as Venetian Francesco da Mosta reminds us, four centuries of Venetian rule as versus a mere 60 by the still ubiquitous Brits.

We fly in
Work to do, people to meet, an Odyssey nonetheless.

Around us, tourists,
Birds of prey fleeing England's dark and rainy summertime.

Together we fall
Toward deep Ionian blue, green hills and olive groves.

Prospero's isle,
Ulysses' last unlikely landing.[1]

---

1 *Identified with Scheria, the island of the Phaeacians (Phaiakians) in Homer's Odyssey, Corfu was settled by Corinthian colonists c. 730 BC. It passed under Roman rule in 229 BC, and in AD 336 became part of the Byzantine Empire. Held by a series of foreign powers, most notably for over four centuries by the Venetian republic, Corfu was ceded to Greece by the British in 1864. It was occupied by the French in World War I. In 1923 Corfu was bombarded and temporarily occupied by Italian forces.*

From Wikipedia: Many ancient and modern interpreters favour identification of Scheria with the island of Corfu, which is within 80 miles of Ithaca. Locals on Corfu had long claimed this, based on the rock outside Corfu harbour, which is supposedly the ship that carried Odysseus back to Ithaca, but was turned to stone by Poseidon, to punish the Phaiakians for helping his enemy: "…with one blow from the flat of his hand turned her [the ship] into stone and rooted her to the sea bottom" (Homer, The Odyssey)

Modern day gods
Greet us: Dionissus, Miranda, Andreas, Simona.

Music of the spheres
Plays round about, we wander in the wizard's wake.

An Austrian
Diverts us on his replica lyre, resurrecting ancient ceramic dreams.

Our magic circle grows:
Alessandro, Johanna, Anatasia. Old gods smile down.

An army of swallows
Drink in insetti. Protected in the evening starlight.

The magic isle
Wraps us round, welcomes us in, whispers old tales come true.

The Phaiakians did not participate in the Trojan War. The Greek word Phaiakians is derived from phaios *meaning grey, hence Phaiakians means "dark-skinned". The Phaiakians in the Odyssey did not know who Odysseus was, so they called him a "stranger". Odysseus however was the king of the majority of the Ionian Islands, not only of Ithaca, but also "of Cephallenia, Neritum, Crocylea, Aegilips, Same and Zacynthus" so if Scheria was Corfu, it would be surprising that the citizens of one of the Ionian Islands did not know Odysseus. Furthermore, when Odysseus introduced himself to Nausikaa he added: "if I outlive this time of sorrow, may become my there guests though I live so far away from all of you" indicating that Scheria was far away from Ithaca. From the ancient times, some scholars having examined the work and the geography of Homer have suggested that Scheria was located in the Atlantic Ocean. Among them were Strabo and Plutarch.*

Approximately eight centuries after Homer, Strabo, the geographer criticized Polybius on the Geography of the Odyssey. Strabo proposed that Scheria and Ogygia were located in the middle of the Atlantic Ocean:
'At another instance he (Polybius) suppresses statements. For Homer says also: "Now after the ship had left the river-stream of Oceanus" and "In the island of Ogygia, where is the navel of the sea," where the daughter of Atlas lives; and again, regarding the Phaiakians, "Far apart we live in the wash of the waves, the farthermost of men, and no other mortals are conversant with us." All these (incidents) clearly suggest that he (Homer) composed them to take place in the Atlantic Ocean.' (Strabo, 1.2.18)

Owl at Day's End
December 31, 2008

Creamy white
Flying low over burnished straw fields
Against black line of bush and tree
Wingspan full of power
The owl at day's end
Said it all

Spoke to me
Of time's passing, how we survived
Black death, one another, ourselves
The White Lady's embrace
Each day its reward
Wrapped up

The black cat
His eyes bright yellow, beast of prey
Below, in the frosty garden
Looking up, who hunts who
Up above I watch
Wondering

Memorial to the poet John Clare in his native village of Helpston (see over)

2009

The Great Returning: Sunwards

*Written for Great Returning Talk
at the Glastonbury Goddess Conference, 1 August 2009*

Around we go
Spinning in Her Light
Moving in Her Spirit
Turning on Her Wheel

Our Time has Come
The Great Returning Commences...

We watch the children wind round Her Bright Form
They touch our hearts
Wise Crones, old and young
Mothers and Queens, Budding Maidens
We welcome in the Workers for Our MotherWorld
Dancing and singing
We all face the Bright Light of a sizzling future

No blame No shame
The time to act is *now* as MotherWorld heats up
Our Bright Will cools and slows the divine dance of the elements
With sunfire witchery Starhawk steps into our Past to plant seeds
Whilst cunning Kathy[1] waves her Magic Wand
One by one the parasites transform to divinites
We command The Day under Sun Mother's Gaze

Our Magic is old, so old we have forgotten
But now we remember our selves
We speak in tongues of fire
Our Bliss wafts skyward as fragrant mists
The Goddesses hear our pleas of praise

We shall overcome

---

1   *Kathy Jones, Goddess Conference convener*

2010

In Memory of John Clare, Fen Poet

On watching David Dimbleby's 'A Picture of Britain: The Flatlands'
18 May 2010

I've hardly read you
But all round me I read through you
Through your despair and joy
I have seen enough to know
A Man of High Heart.

If I had been in your village
When you walked those eighty miles home
To homelessness, away from madness
Seeking respite, I would have
Opened my door and welcomed you in.

Our sky-wide landscape is not for the faint-hearted
Or the unwary, one must choose the right road
And watch the ditch-folds well when night falls
Follow the owls to perch, predators
Fetching home food and succour.

If I read you deeply I will weep well
For the loss of freedoms still out of reach,
Taken from us or never ours to cherish.
You were robust in our defence.
Today perchance we'd do a battle dance

In front of the cameras—your voice
Would stream forth across the peaty soil
And the enclosures would be undone.
We would wake to hope when fen sunlight
Walks long through morn and eventide.
May our souls turn in their eternal rounds
So you can see through time to us and ours.

How Could I Not Love
An English Garden Overmuch?
3 June, 2010

As lilacs pass over, wild geraniums take on the purple
Lavender makes a fast advance as bluebells hit the dust
I make way for over-the-top gladiolas whilst foxgloves
Threaten to make hay while the sun shines
A self-seeded Maple with its magical twin-trunk darkens my window
Protectively covering a mass of long stemmed daisy-types, herbs gone mad,
Wild strawberries, ivy topsy-turvy but an old red rose holds her own.

Meantime, over on the veggie garden patch, all sorts of salads
Demand attention: the wintering-over rainbow chard wins
First prize, a close second to the burgeoning celery plant,
An agro-fen-favourite—like the innumerable beet seedlings
Who make a nuisance of themselves—silly me,
Using their throw-away compost—how could they not claim back
What's naturally theirs, this clay-rich dark fenland soil?

Who manages who, the garden or the gardener?
Pan smiles from around the corner of the arbor
Where the White Goddess holds court, veiled from
Ordinary eyes by a massive overgrowth of white roses and jasmine
Old with scent, Lucy Boston[1] will be proud of me
When she crosses the Threshold to mind matters
Here on this side, her silver slippers leaving tell-tale tracks.

And the trees, the adorable Cherry, more fruitful each year.
A lesson to the slim but fruitless Apricot whose secret
I have not yet divined—ah, the Fig who promises much
But drops its fruit in its determination to grow monster
Fig leaves as if it knows The Fall is coming.
And our careful favourite, out of sight from Sweet Cherry,
The Lemon Tree that produces sunballs all year round.
How could I not love an English Garden overmuch?

---

1 *Noted children's author, whose ancient house is in Hemingford Grey, near St Ives*

Leona and Florence at Madron's Well, Cornwall

Mourning Mother
14 June 2010

Almost six months now. The poems gestate.

I go over my last days with her.
I talk with her everyday.
I talk with others about her.
I miss her.
I cry.
I struggle with the immutable
Truth of Death.

Mom's still there when I need her.
My life is an outworking of some part of her.
She's a reference point on so many fronts.

There's guilt and misery and loss,
So much more one could have done and said,
So many other journeys we could have taken.

Ageing took command.
I am watching myself more carefully,
The way she watched me:
Seize the day, daughter. Burn out, don't rust out.
Old Age is not for the weak or faint of heart.

She died within four months of Ev—
Along with Pat from up the street—
They were her last best pals, the beloved Oakridge Coffee Group.

There were three Evelyns:
Her first best girl pal next door on Garnock Avenue,
Ev and Evelyn from the Phillipines
Who cared for her so lovingly in her last year.

Mom was Sophia, a philosopher,
A woman of words, a voracious reader.
There's something in A Word,
To Name is to divine…
One day suddenly Ev was gone
No service to mourn her. That was hard,
Then Ev's husband Evan in the hospital on the same floor
At the same time as Mom.
He died soon after.
Pat bravely battles on, as does Irene across the road,
And Roy next door.
The Great Generation, spanning two World Wars.

Mother was frail and tired of the battle.
She would have been 96 on 22nd December 2009.
She died 24th November, claiming "It's hard to die."

Roses—red, white, pink and gold—bloom in my English garden.
She would love them but
Maybe disapprove of the black cat who takes it all for granted.

When I clean my sink
I remember long ago, in B.C.,
She'd come to visit and clean my sink.
Now I have a proper Canadian broom
I feel her hands sweeping the dust away.
A woman needs to keep her kitchen reasonable.
But cleaning and dusting became less important
As philosophy took precedence.

She'd figured the money trip out too.
She thought me a spendthrift.
I called it being generous.
We begged to differ.

She was supremely my mother.
Not sure about father.
She gave away a secret but took it back,
Keeping The Family United

As she remembered hers to be when her mother lived
And died when she was fifteen
As the Great Depression came upon them all

What she loved most
Was us all being together, with her,
Drinking tea, eating, laughing
Even arguing, after all, we're bloody Celts.

This isn't the end Mom
Just a new beginning. Keep tuned in.

Leona with her sister Joan, in the backyard of '540', the Graham family's London Ontario homestead

My Sister's Dream
23 June 2010

In my sister's dream
Mother knocks on the door of '540'.
She answers.
Mother says "I've decided to come back'.
Dressed for the cold,
She appears sprightly, years younger
Than when she passed, so frail, so ready to leave.
They hug one another.

At first I was miffed,
Me, family mystic,
That Mom came back to her
After my long vigil there,
Cleaning up, clearing out,
Saying good-bye, making sacred space
For the Family Honour
But now, it seems most meet.

We do live on in Mother's Big Dream.
Where we return to care for her beloved home
On Oakridge Drive in London Ontario
That she worked so hard to keep for us
And if it hadn't been for my sister
Stepping up to the plate so many years ago
It never could have happened.
Mom came back to say you are a good daughter.

She called me 'a good daughter' many times
As she aged unbearably beside me
As we wandered the world
And shopped at the mall
As she grew smaller
But wiser in many ways, understanding age,
Even at the very end on her deathbed.
Being a good daughter was paramount.

Her Mother died when she was fifteen.
Florence always strove to be a good daughter
Like her sister Thelma. 'Saint Nell'.
I used to tease her about Grandmother.
Family first. No matter death.
So we two sisters, we carry on, like it or not,
We must be good daughters, mothers and aunts,
And more to boot, for goodness sake.

Cherry Picking
25 June 2010

Cherry picking in my garden today
It came to mind about that expression:
'Cherry picking':

We choose the riper cherries
If we can find them, the ripest
Unless they've gone off,

Try to get them before the birds do
Or nasty infestations by bugs,
Awaiting their ripening eagerly.

Not much more to be said,
Analogies too obvious to explain,
Except about the sheer glory.

Picking cherries in one's own garden
From one's own cherry tree
At solstice time in a hot English summer

In my bare feet, skimpy dress,
The lavender growing leggy long
Thornless loganberries coming on

The foxgloves climbing to the heavens
Pink and yellow and beyond
Rich white roses weighty from sheer might

The neighbour's yellow roses peeking over
To watch it all, thorny red roses demand it
As the aromatic pink fade away

Everyday the garden spirits call me out
To labour in their wisdom
Picking cherries, the order of the day.

Voices in the Garden
27 June 2010

The day the Germans beat the English
In Bloemfontein, South Africa
To the sound of vuvuzelas...

The lot to the left come from Manchester.
I'm told they're a noisy bunch anyway,
Bloody loud and proud to be.

To the right, two birthdays,
With champagne and football, baby cries
And flags for Middle England.

The hottest day this year, 30 celsius,
Both very English and not.
No complaints, yet.

In between the black cat hides from it all
In deep thicket of white rose and jasmine,
Soundless.

All around this magic fen garden
Birds careen, happy as the day is long
Trilling, enchanting.

Deeper in, behind it all, nature spirits,
Elemental voices, elves and faeries
Singing old tales.

Poetry at the End of the World
29 June 2010

Maybe the end of our world,
The dark at the end of the human tunnel,
Maybe we're finally getting there
After a lot of false shows.

This poem is my sandwich board:
The End is Nigh, we've been very naughty
So the gods will punish us.
So we might as well fly and drive, live dangerously.

We've had a good party.
Those lucky bastards,
The ones who've snuck off recently,
Knowing, pretending their time had come.

Ah, fuck, what a drag,
Doomed humanity and so many other
Species, we're taking them with us,
Right? No one likes going it alone.

Facing it, even with a pretty good life
Under our belt, semi-vegetarian or even vegan,
Is unbelievable torture, how can we sleep?
Things still seem so normal.

So it's all a lie, a climate conspiracy,
But we're all *con-spirators*, we all breathe,
We're all descended from those who
Started it all, we're just ending it.

Maybe. Despite Lovelock's
Prophecy of doom, we look around
At the children, naughty and nice,
We have to have a go.

Approaching sunset at Holywell-cum-Needingworth, Cambridgeshire

We are just making plans,
Making it part of business as usual,
When the Gulf of Mexico disaster blows,
Putting peak oil protests into an interesting perspective.

Some of us hope the mess helps
The Big Mess, raises consciousness,
But BP's stock has fallen to a 14 year low
And British pensions are at risk.

Oh hell, how will we keep up our lifestyles?
And to top it off England lost to Germany
In football and Fabio's career is in doubt.
It's very hard to be serious.

We really must pull ourselves up
And think Victory Gardens,
Tighten our belts for The Coalition .
Maybe it's time to get redundant.

Meantime the G8/20 meet in TO
Where debt, not the end of the world
Is the Big Topic. But they are right,
It is about debt, just The Big Debt.

Maybe the concept of debt and austerity
Will trigger the human instinct of survival
And BP's bloody bureaucracy, like all the others,
Will shatter, and the glass will be empty.

Maybe. But just in case it works out
And somebody's out there, down the line,
I'm writing poetry
At the end of the world.

Canada Day, 2010

For my Canadian Family
1 July 2010

On Canada Day
I rose sluggish to the bright sun
But the garden called
And Hermes[1] was hard at work
Being a cool cat on a hot day.

Made me milky tea,
Coop cornflakes with California walnuts,
Picked cherries for a crumble
And a few bits of rhubarb.
Mary, Mother of Jesus, what a life!

You lot were all still sleeping,
Dreaming of Toronto back to normal[2],
Holidays up in Huntsville,
Wee Geordy—a favourite monster truck, maybe,
Not 1812 or Louis Riel.

I grew up in Pearson's domain,
Now it's just a big airport.
I never voted for Trudeau.
I was always an NDPer.
Still pluggin for Jack[3] as PMer.

O Canada!

---

1 *Our black cat with yellow eyes*
2 *Toronto has been hosting G8/G20 this week, been a bit in shutdown mode downtown, with 'incidents' happening*
3 *Jack Layton, head of NDP & my rep in the Commons.*

But I have a proper broom[1] now
So when I am lonely
I grab it to sweep away sadness,
And make my mom's potato salad.
I'm working up to a cherry pie
Gluten free with home grown fruit
In memory of Florence and her mom,
Mistresses of pies and pastry.
They're together now at Resthaven.[2]

I'm glad to be Canadian.
If one has to be of a nation,
Ours is cool, but of late, lacking
In integrity. My folks all came
From British Isles, so I manage here.

So much yet to be done
To rectify the misuse of power.
It's time to turn it around
And become the inspiration
We think ourselves to be.

First thing, shut down those
Fucking tar sands and stop
Slaughtering seal cubs.
It's really lowered our status.
Our *genii loci* are unhappy.

I wish ye well on our National Day!
I always think it fun
That we nipped in the 1st before the 4th
Upstaging our scary neighbours to the south,
Not that they notice, but it's us who count.

---

1   North American straw broom, unlike UK push brooms.
2   On 21 June 2010, my sister Joan produced a marvelous Memorial at Resthaven Sanctuary in Scarborough (Toronto). My mother had told me that she wanted to be with her mother Nell, who is buried there with her husband John McIntyre Boyd and her first daughter, Aunt Thelma. A plaque now memorializes them all, as well as my brother Ian.

Back to my English idyll now.
Maybe tonight I'll listen to Radio Riel[1]
And dream of heroes, Metis and Mi'Kmaq,[2]
Bonnie Dundee and the Great Montrose.[3]
After all, remember, our Graham motto is: *Ne Oublie*.[4]

Crimepetitive Capitalism[5]
7 July 2010

Michael Moore's movie
'*Capitalism: A Love Story*'.
Marches rampant over hallowed soil,
The American Dream of Sacred Greed
And the Good Life.
He tells a story We in The West
Prefer not to notice:
It doesn't work, it destroys the Middle Class,
Makes Big Rich richer, The Poor poorer,
And throws in The Unbelievable,
Dead Peasant Insurance by Big Business.

Dig in your heels, guys and dolls,
Don't go down without a fight.
Defend your end, hide your oil stocks,

---

1 My husband's and friends' internet radio station, but no connection to 'the' *Riel, the great Metis leader.*
2 Or Micmac: First Nation of Nova Scotia, where I was born in 1942.
3 Graham Ancestors.
4 Sic. See Graham Clan in Wikipedia.
5 Input from my wise cousin, Dr Gary Boyd (Concordia University, Montreal, Canada): "We must distinguish between 'crimepetitive' crapitalism which competes by selling crap and trashing its competitors. vs. 'qualipetitive capitalism' which competes by providing better quality, appropriate (eg. green) goods and services. The five billions who are not starving could not possibly be fed, clothed, sheltered, doctored and educated were it not for qualipetitive (responsible government regulated and moderated) capitalisms."

Demand business as usual.
It's human nature to want more.

Die believing it lest ye wake to it.
No better than communism that never was
Or socialism that would be.
All systems corrupt in human hands.
Another toy, another bomb, another enemy.
It's true, systems suck.

Human bozos will always create box-isms,
Solutions become traps,
Mazes for the cheesy-minded.
Then we unmake, madly, deeply,
Swing over to revolution,
Red guards to black shirts
And brightly coloured flags.
Until one day we'll get it,
None too soon, and then wonder
Why we did it, such primitive behaviour.
And the white rose battles with jasmine in my country garden.

Shades of Green
14 July 2010

Today
The Angel Said
Count yourself lucky,
A good life, a good husband, a great garden,
The list went on.

I sit now
In the mornings
Propped up on pillows in my big bed
Perusing the skyline across the fens,
The shades of green trees make.

It came to pass
In this one small life
Not fortune or fame,
I am indeed lucky,
But Something Good:

A life lived to the full,
Knowing finally contentment
Along with Weltschmerz,
The suspension bridge across,
Like one crossed in childhood, across another Thames[1].

I am part of the small work[2]
As well as The Big.
When called, I come,
Hands ready, at arms, at ease.
Once upon a time I was a Leading Wren.

---

1 London, Ontario, Canada. Suspension bridge across the Thames at the Thames Country Golf Course near Oakridge Acres where I grew up in the late Fifties and Sixties.
2 The One Work, in this case, spiritual-cum-environmental

Cloudbank Across the Fens

Now, Gaia sings Her Lament
And we trudge behind,
Her long row of soldiers
Bearing forks and spades
To clean up The Mess
We have made.

We come in shades of green
And Pan howls in the shadows.
I murmur something about Findhorn
And His Green Eyes pop out:
None too soon, sweetheart.

Ah, shit, how will we manage
Without A Re-enchantment of the World?
Bloody hard work
Even with Bloom[1] on the case
With other modern magicians.

The lavender blossoms
In my Victory Garden;
The bees rebound and the dragonflies dart.
Hermes the yellow-eyed black prince
Surveys our domain. Content.

---

1   William Bloom of Glastonbury, teacher & author.

Woman Waiting For A Bus In Oxford
20 July 2010

She, me, myself
Waiting for a bus
Woman of an age…

We've let our hair go
White, haloed in the right light
Loose-limbed

Beige trews[1], sandals
Ethnic bag[2]
She's me, here in Oxford

Except I didn't
Take this route
To The Academic Mecca

I just pop in to visit
Old friends who did,
Busy and immersed.

Just a vague fleeting
Regret, but then
She's here, instead

For me and all the gals
Who didn't,
Who flew the coop

Took to The Road,
Talked to The Fairies
And Courted Chaos.

---

1   *Somewhat archaic Brit colloquial for trousers.*
2   *All the rage, eh, once agin?*

She climbs on The Bus
For Us, restless in
Her harness of purple

She, me, we, us,
Chorus girls for The World:
We will, we can, we did.

Women On The Bus
Going Somewhere,
Ageing Wonderfully Well.

The Call of Isis
20 August 2010

Q: Goddess of Old, whence, whereto do You call The Querent?

A: Down Paths of The Unforgettable,
Beyond dreary tomes and tombs
Of modern day macabre.

Follow the Fellowship of Isis[1].
Weary not, My footsteps
Well light The Way.

Re-member the Mystery,
Stars shine through
Cloud, rain, moon and sunbow.

Q: How shall This Querent find you?

A: Elen of the Trackways[2]
Riding Her night-mare
Snags Her prey

---

1   FOI: *The Fellowship of Isis*: co-founded by Lady Olivia Durdin-Robertson, now 92. Lady Olivia's autobiographical work is called **The Call of Isis**.
2   In the 1980's Caroline Wise made the world more aware of this ancient Welsh Goddess, naming Her Elen of the Ways; we eagerly await her book on Elen!

2010

Climbs the stars
To bring you home to Me
Mother of All

Stretched across the skies.
Her reins skeins of gold
Silver horned in the moonlight.

Q: What awaits The Querent at The End of Her Journey?

A: Here, at Home with The Holy Ones
We remake Our Selves
Through Their Eyes we see through.

The First Mystery is our Ignorance.
Sloughed off, the gilded snake
Returns, wrapped around Our Bliss.

There is Work to do.
Come hence.
Tarry not.

A Year On
From Florence's Passing
2 December 2010

I imagine
Which is real
She speaks to me
Now and then

Gives me good advice
As always
And lends me her strong arm up
Into righteousness

She lives deep within me
Now she walks with me
The truest love must out
Her passion for life blossoms bright

In all her children, grand and great grand children
Even in the memory of one gone
Ahead of the rest.
A true Matriarch of the First Order.

2011

Isis Unveiled, Insh'Allah

A Response to the Revolutions in North Africa and the Gulf States
2 March 2011

She reveals Herself to us
As Her ancient homelands
Erupt in revolution

She speaks through
Many mouths
One truth

They do not call Her Name
But when they call His
She is also there

Faces bared or covered
Arms naked or clothed
Hands raised as one

The March to Freedom
In Her Old Lands
Is His March too

Man and woman, child and adult,
One Spirit, encompassing religion,
Spirituality in the yearning for freedom

And yes, Death stalks the sands
Pours out upon the streets
And the wailing of the women in black

Tears my heart
For the wild children of Freedom's Call
We sit in the waiting room

Over in the so-called West
Watching the fabled East
With trepidation

Where our mutual sun always rises
Where the moon symbolizes beauty
Where Red Cross and Crescent Moon

Side by side on the Tunisian border
Serve The People
Sharing an old history

We must look up and back
And inward, around and through
To understand where we must stand

The pain, the agony, the torture
Of needs unmet for too long
Human together we shall sing

The Song of Freedom
Hope in Our Time
To hell with vested interests

Just this once, forever,
Can we get it right
All of us

As we face the even greater battle
Ahead, as winds and seas,
The very substance of earth

Also demand justice,
An intelligent response
From a liberated species

www.ingramcontent.com/pod-product-compliance
Lightning Source LLC
LaVergne TN
LVHW011215080426
835508LV00007B/802